What do you want to know about Halloween?

AROUND THE WORLD

Today, Halloween is on October 31st and November 1st in many countries.

In Canada and the US, children dress up and ask for candy. Trick or treat!

In Santiago Sacatepeques, Guatemala, people fly big, beautiful kites.

In Ireland, children play games and eat Barn Brack, a fruit bread.

In Hong Kong, children dress up and have parties.

The Story of Halloween

Long ago in Britain, farmers finished their work on
October 31st when winter came.
The next day, November 1st, was the Festival of the Dead.

This was the day when the ghosts of dead people came. Farmers were scared and tried to trick the ghosts. They painted their faces and made big fires.

The other name for November 1st is
All Hallows Day.

The evening before All Hallows Day is
All Hallows Evening.

Most people call All Hallows Evening
by the name Halloween.

ALL HALLOW'S EVENING

HALLOW E EN

Jack O'Lanterns

Happy eyes, a silly nose
A funny mouth, long green toes.
Ugly, terrible, scary!
Fat, round, hairy!
Big, small, short and tall,
Jack O'Lanterns for one and all!

A MAGIC SPELL

It was a cold, dark Halloween night.
The children were trick or treating for candy.
Wilma Witch was angry.

"Those children!
I want some candy too!
I will turn them into
frogs!" She made a
magic spell.

"One cat's ear, two black spiders,

a crocodile's tooth, and an old dirty sock"

··· sszzzsszzsszzzsszzzz!

···YOU turned into a frog!
You said, "Ribbit!" and jumped.

···And Wilma Witch ate all
your Halloween candy!

Please come to a
HALLOWEEN PARTY!

When? _ _ _ _ _ _ _ _

What time? _ _ _ _ _ _ _ _

Where? _ _ _ _ _ _ _ _

Play games! Listen to ghost stories!
Eat monster's hair and eyes, ➜

black spiders,

witches' fingers,

➜

⬅ snake juice

and Halloween candy!

MOVIE MAGIC

Here is Harry Potter at school.

This is his teacher.

Gandalf and Frodo are from 'The Lord of the Rings.'

TRICK OR TREAT

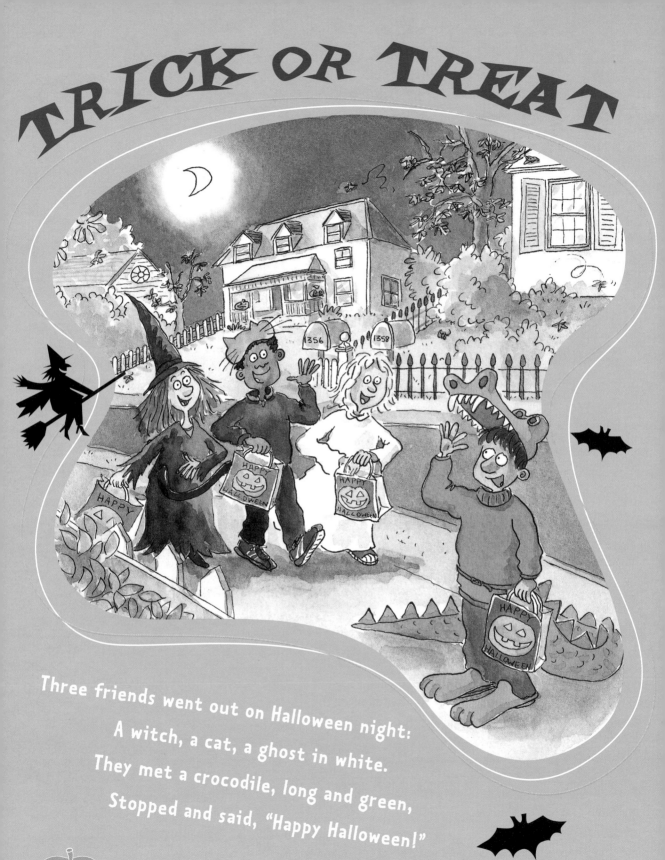

Three friends went out on Halloween night:
A witch, a cat, a ghost in white.
They met a crocodile, long and green,
Stopped and said, "Happy Halloween!"

12

They came to a house with a monster's head,
And all four friends stood and said,
"Trick or treat! Trick or treat!
Give me something good to eat!"

The door opened … nobody was there …
The four children had a scare!
They ran to the next house in the street.
"Trick or treat! Trick or treat!"

ACTIVITIES

Before You Read

1. Look at the pictures in the book. Can you find:

   something scary?   something to eat?

   something that flies?   an animal?

   some fruit?

After You Read

2. Look at the picture on page 7.

   (a) How many Jack O'Lanterns can you see?

   (b) Can you find the:

   silly nose

   long green toes

   funny hair

   two oranges?

3. Look in the book. Are these sentences true or false?

   (a) In the US, people fly kites on Halloween.

   (b) In Britain, people made big fires on November 1st.

   (c) Halloween is the evening before All Hallows Day.

   (d) In Hong Kong, children eat fruit bread on Halloween.

   (e) Wilma Witch was angry.

   (f) On Halloween people say "Trick and Treat!"

Pearson Education Limited
Edinburgh Gate, Harlow
Essex CM20 2JE, England
and Associated Companies throughout the world.

ISBN 0582 778573

First published by
Penguin Books 2003

1 3 5 7 9 10 8 6 4 2

Text copyright © Margaret Lo 2003
Illustrations © Rhian Nest James/Kathy Jakeman, pages 7 and 10;
Derek Brazell/Artist Partners, pages 8-10; Judy Brown, pages 12-14

Photos are reproduced by courtesy of:
Corbis, pages 2, 3 (top); Foodfeatures (centre), Associated Press;
Mary Evans Picture Library, pages 4-5; DK Library, page 10;
Pictorial Press, page 11, © Warner Brothers (top) and UA/Fantasy (below)

The moral rights of the author and illustrators have been asserted

Halloween, Level 2
Series Editor: Melanie Williams
Series created by Annie Hughes and Melanie Williams
Design by John Fordham
Color reproduction by Spectrum Colour, Ipswich
Printed in Great Britain by Scotprint, Haddington

Published by Pearson Education Limited in association with Penguin Books Ltd, both
companies being subsidiaries of Pearson Plc

For a complete list of the titles available in the Penguin Young Readers series
please write to your local Pearson Education office or contact: Penguin Readers Marketing,
Pearson Education, Edinburgh Gate, Harlow, Essex, CM20 2JE

Answers to the Activities in this book are published in the free Penguin Young Readers
Factsheet on the website, www.penguinreaders.com